HAS
BRITAIN
GONE
BONKERS?

First published 2010

The History Press
The Mill, Brimscombe Port
Stroud, Gloucestershire, GL5 2QG
www.thehistorypress.co.uk

British Library Cataloguing in Publication Data.
A catalogue record for this book is available from the British Library.

ISBN 978 0 7524 5711 6

Typesetting and origination by The History Press
Manufacturing managed by Jellyfish Print Solutions Ltd
Printed in India

HAS BRITAIN GONE BONKERS?

CHRIS MARTIN

WHERE DID IT ALL GO WRONG?

For over a century, Britain ruled the largest empire the world has ever known. A quarter of the world's population looked to London as the centre of their universe. British engineering powered this world; our art, cuisine and culture informed it, and it was governed by a legal system underpinned by impeccable British values of fair play and decency.

So what the hell happened?

These days Britain rules the smallest empire the world has ever known including a penguin sanctuary in the South Atlantic, a monkey sanctuary in Spain and the most useless bit of the Antarctic. British engineering is all but non-existent. The last time we made a car the doors rusted off before it got out of the showroom, which is just as well because you can't drive above 5mph on our roads without ploughing into a set of roadworks or getting fined by a speed camera.

Our homes are filled with baffling Chinese-made electronics and our bellies are full of Dixie Fried American Rat Burger. *Celebrity Big Brother* forms the apogee of a British cultural experience which revolves around alcopops, street fights and takeaway curry.

You can forget about fair play and decency – between bankers trousering six-figure bonuses, ASBO grandmothers with their pit bull justice, footballers in Armani thongs and MPs blowing their expenses on duck houses we haven't got a chance.

In a world driven mad by local council legislation where the people have been enslaved by health and safety Stalins in high-visibility gillets, we are left asking the question: Has Britain Gone Bonkers?

SAT NAV SLAVERY

Man had been successfully using maps to navigate across the face of the planet for 400 years before Jesus invented the Christmas tree. So why on Earth would anyone want to shell out £200 for a bleeping box with the voice of 'Sean', a heavily sedated Irish call centre monkey, to tell them which way to go to the off licence? Five times more difficult to operate than the Large Hadron Collider and about half as useful, the primary purpose of these hi-tech guidance systems seems to be to generate some kind of imbecility wave that causes blind obedience in even the most experienced of drivers.

The latest in an endless series of incomprehensible Sat Nav

blunders saw a 6ft-wide ASDA delivery van squeezing down a heavily-wooded public footpath near Rosendale, Lancashire. Eventually the blundering white van man had to abandon his vehicle when it became wedged in the 3ft-wide path and wait patiently to be towed free by the RAC.

EMPTY BUS LANES

It's hard to deny the streets of our cities are congested and the situation appears to be getting worse. So it would stand to reason that, if people want to move quickly about their business, the local council would supply a road network with room for more cars. What you wouldn't expect them to do is cordon off half the highway for the exclusive use of half-empty buses taking ASBO teenagers to the job centre, self-righteous cyclists in testicle-hugging shorts and homosexuals on Italian mopeds.

Maybe councils would have more money for tarmac if they didn't spend their entire annual budget policing these bus lanes with the kind of surveillance gear that would give a KGB spymaster raging tumescence. Still, that would mean they could no longer issue penalty notices to anyone who pulls over to pick up their dry cleaning or swerves to avoid having their passenger door torn off by the back end of a bendy bus.

These penalty notices have even caught up with the mighty Google; when a camera car photographing local highways for use on Street View was itself captured on camera in a bus lane and fined.

LESSER-SPOTTED DICK

Great Britain is a green and pleasant land and at its throbbing cholesterol-choked heart is traditional British food. Roast beef, Yorkshire pudding, fish 'n' chips and chicken tikka masala are as much of a monument to the British way of life as Nelson's Column or Jodie Marsh's jubblies. So why are the powers that be trying to rename our classic puds to avoid embarrassment?

Most infamously, Flintshire County Council felt the need to change the name of 'Spotted Dick' to 'Spotted Richard' as canteen staff apparently got tired of the giggles and smutty comments made by diners. And they're not the only ones getting all po-faced over some perfectly innocent *Carry-On* humour. In 2001, Tesco also tried change the pudding's name to 'Spotted Richard'. Other variations on the title have included 'Sultana Sponge', 'Spotted Dog' and the frankly ridiculous 'Blemished Richard'.

MALE PREENING

There was a time when men were men and women were women. Traditionally, it was women who led the charge to the bathroom They spent hours at the hairdresser, doused themselves in celebrity-endorsed smellies and kept up with the latest fashions by reading magazines that looked like a laminated version of a Thomson local directory. Meanwhile the sole contribution of men to personal grooming was occasionally splashing water on their faces and smelling the underarms of yesterday's T-shirt to ascertain if it was still wearable.

Not any more. According to business analysts Mintel, the UK market for male personal grooming products is now worth over

£700m. And – if we believe Superdrug's marketing department – a significant proportion of this cash has will be spent on their new range of 'guy-liner'.

Even worse, man-bags – traditionally the preserve of the bi-curious Euro male – are now increasing prevalent on these shores. A man should have a wallet which goes in his pocket or a briefcase that contains work. Anything made from soft leather that can swing from your wrist is frankly unnatural.

Ironically it took an American, the tennis player Andy Roddick, to lay down the lay for British men when he wrote in his blog: 'Anything bigger than a money clip or a wallet is to be left with your girlfriend/wife. And just so we are clear, you should not be able to throw your "wallet" over a shoulder.'

TOBACCO PROHIBITION

Not content with taking half your money in tax that they then spend on cleaning their duck ponds, the Government seems intent on carrying its war on smoking into every aspect of our lives.

The Times reported that self-employed painter and decorator Gordon Williams had been fined £30 by officials

from Ceredigion Council in Wales for smoking in his own van because it is classified as a workplace. Mr Williams said: 'I was on my way to a shop to buy some teabags when the council official pulled me over. I was told that because my van is my place of work I had broken the smoking laws. I am dumbfounded. It is not my place of work. I decorate houses, not vans. I don't use it for work so I can't see how they can do me for smoking in the workplace.'

PARKING

Compared to those of Bogotá or Tehran, the roads in British cities are in pretty good shape. Unfortunately you'd be a fool to use them because there's absolutely nowhere you can park your car. If you do find a space it seems invariably to be designed for a midget in a Peel P50 or decked out with a baffling array of variable restrictions communicated with the kind of florescent signage you would have expected to find at a rave *circa* 1993. Just once, wouldn't it be nice to make a trip to the newsagent to pick up a paper and a packet of Polos without returning to your car to find a Nigerian man in a South American general's uniform writing you a ticket for £60?

Even if you can find a 3-ft gap to squeeze your Volvo into it may not put you beyond the reach of the parking Gestapo. In 2001 parking attendants in Islington turned up with cans of yellow spray paint and, without warning, marked yellow lines around and underneath cars before issuing tickets! A spokeswoman for Islington Council was reported as saying: 'It is the council's duty to refresh the road markings but it is not our policy to paint lines around cars and issue tickets whilst the paint is still wet.' She added: 'We would always wait until the following day to give people a chance to move their cars.'

TERRIBLE PEOPLE CARRIERS

Ever since a French designer decided that crossing a car with a bus might be good idea and sent us the Renault Espace, people carriers have blighted our roads. These monuments to neutered masculinity now account for one in 50 of all new cars bought in the UK.

When a man pulls out onto the highway in this hideous love child of a biscuit tin and a Homebase greenhouse, he makes it clear he's largely given up on life, choosing instead to pilot a screaming mobile holding pen for delinquent children around an over-congested city centre while dreaming of an early, painless death.

Ironically he may not have much longer to wait as these family motors are also incredibly dangerous. The Chrysler Voyager, the USS *Nimitz* of minivans and Britain's second-biggest-selling people carrier, achieved an execrable score of 19 per cent in the front impact tests conducted by EuroNCAP – the European New Car Assessment Programme – which means you may as well be using tissue paper and strong language to protect yourself when you plough into a Range Rover at 70mph.

RAMBLING NONSENSE

Chief among our least-loved social sub-species are 'ramblers'. Not to be confused with the cottager and the dogger (both of whom also enjoy loitering with intent in areas of natural beauty) the rambler is distinguished by his vocal campaigning for his 'right' to 'roam', whether it be through someone's back garden, a Sainbury's car park or down range on Salisbury Plain.

In 2002 rock-and-roll cadaver and part-time guitarist Keith Richards angered ramblers when he launched an unsuccessful campaign to change the route of a footpath across his land which an army of cagoule-clad buffoons was using to walk within 11 yards of his front door. In 2004 Madonna took it a step further, winning the right to stop ramblers walking on her estate by claiming there was a genuine risk they could be shot – presumably by her. Meanwhile, a man who attempted to ramble naked around Britain got just two weeks in jail and a new set of clothes courtesy of the taxpayer.

LOCO PARENTIS

Children are noisy, messy and have a gift for spending money that would make them the envy of any self respecting WAG. It's no wonder we spend so much time hiding from them. However it's one thing to lock yourself in the shed during your daughter's fifth birthday party and another to have council busybodies ban you from your own back yard.

In 2009, Watford council banned parents from playing with their own children in council recreation areas because they had not been vetted by police. Children as young as five were instead to be supervised by council 'play rangers' who had been cleared by the Criminal

Records Bureau. Doleful mothers and fathers were forced to watch their children from outside specially-constructed perimeter fences protecting the two adventure playgrounds unless they had undergone a criminal record check to prove they were not paedophiles.

Despite being branded a disgrace by parents, councillors insisted they were merely following government regulations which did not allow adults to walk around playgrounds 'unchecked'.

TRAFFIC WARDENS

It takes a special kind of person to be a traffic warden. What other job requires the holder to be possessed with the ability to move seamlessly through time and space to appear from nowhere and issue a ticket literally nanoseconds after a meter runs out?

All traffic wardens – sorry, parking attendants – share a suicidal dedication to the intransigent execution of their duty and the letter of the law even when it defies sense to do so. Witness the Manchester bus driver who pulled over to pick up a queue of people only to discover a meter monster finishing a ticket at the back of the line. He and his passengers looked on in disbelief as the warden attached a

£40 penalty notice to the bus for 'Parking in a restricted area'. An honourable mention also goes to the Lambeth parking Nazi who attached a £100 ticket to the crashed scooter of a man who was still lying in the road nearby with a broken leg.

Amazingly you don't even have to be driving a motor vehicle to get a ticket if you live in Yorkshire. When Robert McFarland, a retired blacksmith, left his horse Charlie Boy unattended for a few brief moments, he returned to find a ticket attached to the saddle. Written in the vehicle description was simply 'brown horse'.

THE TALIBAN OCCUPATION OF NORFOLK

There are fewer than a million people living in Norfolk (if you ignore the 2 million illegal turkey pluckers from Eastern Europe who managed to get into the county in the back of a lorry). It is Britain's vegetable garden, home to spectacular fenland, wide sweeping beaches and dribbling yokels with their eyes set a little too close together. Of course most of us will never enjoy this natural beauty – because after having spent three hours trapped behind a muck spreader we'll give up just after Ely and head back to civilisation.

Indeed the sheer inaccessibly of Norfolk by car has gone a long way towards forming its unique character. With its complex network of A-roads permanently clogged by tractors and caravans, the county remains largely inaccessible to road traffic for most of the year. In fact you're better to fly there. From Holland.

On the plus side, the isolation of the place has made it a popular second home location for those too lazy to brave budget flights to Tuscany; on the downside most of its indigenous inhabitants are about as sane as a box of frogs and are often lacking the full complement of grandparents. If a toothless simpleton marrying his first cousin can be considered 'normal for Norfolk' it's not surprising that no-one batted an eyelid when a full-sized Afghan village was knocked up just outside Thetford.

The village in question comes complete with straw-covered streets, donkey-drawn carts and single-storey stone houses populated by 60

Afghans and more than 100 retired Ghurkas who play the part of villagers, Taliban insurgents and Afghan security forces. The site is designed to prepare soldiers for deployment to Afghanistan. A master-stroke by MoD mandarins who realised only in the usually empty Norfolk countryside could a suicide bomber blow himself up with few more consequences than scaring some livestock. The latter, after all, have undoubtedly been through far worse at the hands of the locals.

THE INTERNET

The experienced techno boffins whose place it is to monitor such things recently made the monstrous assertion that 12 per cent of the Internet consists of pornography. Now anyone who actually uses the Internet will tell you this is patently not true – these 'researchers' are obviously missing out on the good stuff.

But even if the Internet is only 12 per cent eye-popping euro-smut and insatiable Japanese nurses then the rest of it is hardly Shakespearean discourse; Mexican Viagra pharmacies, strobe-powered online casinos and Britney Spears fan sites seem to take up around 80 per cent of the whole. This leaves around 8 per cent for the rest of us (cough) to plough through endless pages of contradictory information about swine flu and to compare our current contents insurance with 10,000 competitive quotes.

In 2009 all hope that the greatest technical innovation of our age might be in safer hands with a younger, more digitally adept generation were dispelled when a hapless 17-year-old from Farnborough advertised the party he was hosting in his parents' house on Facebook while they were away. Some 150 gatecrashers arrived at the event which subsequently required 70 police officers, several dogs and a helicopter to suppress the drunken street riot that ensued.

On paper the internet is a powerful research tool. Unfortunately this tool also allows you to be distracted from doing any work whatsoever by looking at naked ladies in the privacy of your own study for hours on end; an activity which would have you barred from your local library.

TWO-WHEEL TERROR

The modern cyclist is a peculiar beast. With their Lycra shorts, high visibility vests and pointy plastic helmets they seem to be in love with the kind of clothing that would make the Artist Formerly Known as Prince blush with embarrassment. That in itself is not crime. Nor is their endless whingeing about the environment going all melty. Even their self-righteous commitment to personal fitness falls flat when most of us would rather Fray Bentos and Ronald McDonald clog our arteries than we be seen in a skin-tight undergarment.

What is a crime however is the sweaty imbeciles' patent disregard for the laws of the highway. A cyclist at high speed is likely to ignore traffic lights, pedestrian crossings, women pushing prams and nuns pushing 90. They are as at home on the pavement as they are in bus lanes and on footpaths; turn your back for a second and they'll plough through even the densest of bus queues with all the restraint of a pubescent boy let loose in a bra factory.

Almost every motorist has felt their head bump off the dashboard after jamming on the brakes to avoid one of these pedal-powered kamikaze pilots, and probably got a mouthful of abuse for their trouble.

PHONEY CONVENIENCE

There are some 71 million mobile phone handsets in the UK. That's around one and a half handsets for every man and woman in the country. Much like the women of Britain, these machines come in all shapes, sizes and colours and some are easier to get into than others. Nowadays your mobile phone allows you to take pictures, access the Internet, remember your kids' birthdays, book restaurants, pay for parking, get your back rubbed and a thousand other useless things you never knew you needed until the salesman suggested you did.

We're told that the modern mobile has more computing power than the Apollo 11 lunar module that put Neil Armstrong on the moon. In fact these digital marvels can do just about everything except make a phone call. When you call your wife to tell her that you've just spent £300 on a new phone from the showroom it sounds like you're in the next room but when you get home and your wife is in the next room it sounds like she's in a showroom. Under water. On the moon.

Unsurprisingly the mobile phone industry's solution has not been to fix our phone reception; instead they've been paying the Government millions for the right to add video calls. The chance of this working when you can't get audio reception outside the M25 is virtually nil. Besides – who wants to be seen by someone when most of us are bleary-eyed, furry-tongued and unshaven in the morning and spend our nights slumped in front of the TV chugging Doritos? More importantly, how will we call in sick to work when the party we went to the night before is still raging in the background behind us?

RUBBISH RECYCLING

Putting out the rubbish used to be easy. All you had to do was remember what day the bin man came then bung everything you didn't want in a black bag and put it out the night before. Not any more. Now we have to plough mercilessly through our own stinking refuse separating cans from tea bags, ear buds from curry containers and newspapers from God knows what else has grown in the depths of the bin over the week. Then we have to decide whether a milk carton half full of potato peel, coffee grains and cigarette butts goes in an orange bag or a black bag before we put it in the green bin or the black bin or the blue bin or possibly even the green basket if its still attached to piece of newspaper with some chewing gum.

As most us of don't have a PhD in waste disposal the bin man has come and gone by the time we make up our minds. The end result is that our single greatest contribution to recycling is having to pay the fine for leaving an apple core next to a bean tin in last week's garbage. Thanks to the Green Gestapo, the crime of placing the wrong vegetable in the wrong bin is now regarded as being on a par with a mass murderer wearing a floor-length kitten skin coat to a children's nativity play.

In 2009 59.9 per cent of our rubbish went to landfill and the rest got sold to China. The latter fact seems ironic as half the packaging, white goods and plastic mugs that we throw away were made in China in the first place.

WAYNE ROONEY

There was a time when someone who played football for living was a working class chap who devoted his life to the game for four shillings a week and was happy when his testimonial match earned him enough to buy a used van to start a second career as a rat catcher. However the advent of the Premiership has reinvented those who sole contribution to civilisation is the ability to kick a ball as vacuous lifestyle brand that owes more to P Diddy than to Bobby Charlton.

Take Wayne Rooney. While undoubtedly a talented player, court papers published during a legal spat with his agents in 2008 revealed that on top of his £90,000-a-week basic wage the Shrek-faced striker earned an extra £760,000 every six months for image rights and a cool £1m a year from Nike. Amazingly the publishers HarperCollins also paid him a whopping £3.55 million as part of a five-book deal documenting his life (eg born, kicked a ball, didn't get caught with a geriatric prostitute – hello lawyers! kicked a ball, died).

His free-spending wife Coleen – who couldn't trap a long cross from midfield to save her life – merited a £283,334 for her eight-book deal (eg born, went shopping, died) and takes home £41,667 a month for her column in *OK* about – you guessed it – shopping. That's a lot of cash to spend on pink Bentleys, plastic surgery and diamond encrusted trainers.

And what do the youth of today get to aspire to from these latter-day heroes of the hallowed turf? Their smell. Following David and

Victoria Beckham's foray into the world of perfumery, for a trifling £35 you can now purchase *Coleen X* and smell just like the lady herself. At the time of publication there are no plans to release a perfume that smells like Wayne.

CHASING GINGERS

The need to hunt and gather is hard-wired into even the most beer bellied, sofa surfing telly addict among us. Our ability to bear down on the remote control or follow the scent of a slice of cold pizza that has fallen down the back of the sofa are gifts from our cave-dwelling ancestors. A West Country pub, with moth eaten stag head above the fireplace and jolly nineteenth-century prints on the wall, is a veritable shrine to a pursuit as essential to the rural way of life as cousin marriage and dead dog cider.

The first modern ban on hunting with hounds was introduced in Germany in 1933 – and if that date seems familiar, it's not a coincidence.

The edict was extended to Austria in 1938 by the same group of animal lovers. Says Bernd Ergert of Munich's hunting museum: 'The aristocrats were understandably furious, but they could do nothing about the ban given the totalitarian nature of the regime'. Plus ça change. In 2004 New Labour's ban on the ancient pastime of fox hunting sought to legislate against yet another of our age-old freedoms.

But given that it's impossible to outlaw riding a horse while wearing a red coat and exercising one's hounds, that legislation has proved remarkably ineffective. And with one beleaguered rozzer and his Land Rover for every 200 square miles of countryside, a piece of legislation debated for longer in the House of Commons than the invasion of Iraq has had little effect.

While driving a horse through a freezing cold peat bog for two hours on the off chance of seeing a large animal bite the head off a smaller one might not be everyone's cup of tea it's certainly our right to do it. Ban fox hunting and before you know it you will need a license from Brussels to change a light bulb in your own home.

INFAMOUS LIVING

There was a time when the greatest perk of celebrity was your mother telling her friends at bingo that you were on the television and the chance to be insulted by the Duke of Edinburgh at the Royal Variety Performance. Nowadays even the briefest and most undistinguished appearance on the idiot box seems to open the door to a golden world of untold riches, supermodel dating and roast albatross dinners at The Ivy.

It is the advertisers who are to blame for this risible situation having rendered us quite incapable of buying anything without a celebrity endorsement. As a result Richard Hammond tells us where to shop, Gary Lineker tells us what crisps to eat and Bill Wyman has his own signature metal detector. If Pauline Quirke advertised pile cream we'd all be down the doctor's the next day to get our grapes anointed.

Perversely the telly itself is now dependent on celebrity patronage to survive with tired old shows being recycled with the magic dust of celebrity. *Celebrity Big Brother* or *Celebrity Fat Club* have all limped on thanks the 'Z' list magic of George Galloway and Rick Waller.

Celebrities would like us to think that they have ordinary lives. Well they don't and we don't want them to. We want to know that the price of fame is having your every waking second recorded through a telephoto lens by man in anorak who lives in his car.

We should ensure only those who have made a contribution to the nation will profit from advertising; henceforth General Sir Mike Jackson will replace Jamie Oliver as the face of Sainsbury's. Iceland may continue to use Kerry Katona.

HOT AIR

When they've finished ranting till the veins on their temples throb like angry boa constrictors, the fog-horn voiced tree huggers would have us cover every square inch of the countryside with wind turbines. Hugely expensive, 100 feet high and capable of generating enough electricity to make a cup of tea in Wales, it has never been exactly clear whom these monuments to eco-stupidity are helping.

Driving past a wind farm at speed, the slowly turning rotors do have a certain beauty. However, having what amounts to a gigantic mincer for birds on your doorstep is hardly ideal. That's not to mention the bats. A six-week study at a wind farm in the eastern United States recorded 2,900 bat fatalities. And bat fatalities outnumber bird deaths by two to one.

More worryingly, wind farms may drive us all mad. Another US survey found the turbines in Ohio were causing 'mental illness' and psychological problems among nearby residents. The reason for this was the constant 'thrumming' noise the blades make as they rotate. So wind farms are great news if you don't live near them, like tea and are not a winged mammal. Everyone else has a simple choice – get driven mad by eco-nagging or be sent to the funny farm because of the constant humming.

REVOLTING STUDENTS

Whatever happened to student protest? Wouldn't it be nice to see today's students get off their Playstations and back to protesting about real issues like war and civil liberties? Thanks to the divine mission of his royal Tonyness and his New Labour cronies we now require a permit to open a packet of crisps near a school and Britain been locked in a decade-long war against an enemy so unseen that we may as well be fighting Lord Lucan; yet there's not a peep from campus.

In the Sixties and Seventies, British students led the world in dressing in stupid hats and big boots while skipping lectures to experiment with soft drugs and hard rock. They protested about everything from animal rights to the price of a pint in the student union. Today's lot seem content to keep their heads down for three years in the effort to get grades good enough to stroll into an entry level position at KPMG.

Rubbish though today's students are there may be larger factors at work here. Half a million people turned out to protest fruitlessly against the invasion of Iraq and a million wasted their time marching down in the Mall to support their right to enjoy animal genocide in their leisure time. Could it be that no-one actually believes that protest really works?

ROADWORKS

The M25 was conceived in 1937 but it was another 50 years before the London Orbital was opened to the motoring public. On that proud day in 1986 the road immediately exceeded its capacity and gave birth to its first tailback. By 1993 the road, which was originally designed to carry 88,000 cars a day, was heaving under the weight of 200,000 and the Government decided it was time to get the cones out. There has been roadworks-related congestion on some part of the M25 every day ever since.

Contraflows, narrow lanes, chicanes and camera-enforced average-speed zones are as much part of the UK's road network as

Little Chefs and bundles of discarded pornography in lay-bys. It's got to the point where most drivers would actually find it hard to believe they were on a motorway unless they were crawling along at 5mph through a 14-mile rat run of speed humps, ill assembled signage and discard tarmac rollers.

Ironically, a 2006 survey by the AA Motoring Trust declared the UK roadworks to be some of the best in Europe; though they declined to explain their criteria for this award. Perhaps then we should be proud of the density and sheer inevitability of our roadworks system. When travelling around Europe it is possible to drive clear across some countries and not see so much as a temporary traffic light. In Britain you're lucky to pull out of your driveway without having to navigate through traffic calming measures or wait for a bored-looking Albanian in a hard hat to flip a tin sign.

CONCORDE

When Concorde passed overhead it froze time. Builders stopped whistling at schoolgirls, traffic wardens stopped writing tickets and old ladies stopped doing bugger all to look skywards and marvel at the beauty of the world's first supersonic passenger airliner.

Concorde was responsible for a slew of records which still haven't been surpassed, including the fastest transatlantic flight (two hours, 52 minutes from take-off to touchdown) and the fastest time around the World (32 hours and 49 minutes, including refuelling stops). When it was finally retired Concorde had clocked up nearly a million flight hours over 27 distinguished years. And better still this miracle of technology was British (with some help from the French, who mostly took care of the catering and the uniforms).

Despite being years ahead of its time, in 1999 the plane was scrapped and the progress of mankind took a huge leap backwards. Thanks to the efforts of the bean counters in the Government and their equally short-sighted friends at the airlines rather than get to the States in three hours in comfort, we now have to spend nine hours wedged between two massively fat Texans in a seat that Kate Moss could barely get a buttock on.

iPODS

It's the question of the modern age – do I need an iPod? Well, if you can summon the patience to read the instruction manual, you're not put off by a control panel that would be more at home on the Starship *Enterprise* and your fingers aren't too fat to work the buttons it could be pretty useful. And let's face it, thanks to the proliferation of electronic gizmos, such things are no longer the preserve of desperate bachelors and Japanese schoolchildren.

You would have thought that the cutting edge of a revolution in micro-electronics would be in kidney dialysis machines or space travel but it's not; it's music. Not a day goes past without some new music player being advertised on the goggle box by beaming teenagers prancing through a shopping centre in New York or Milan.

The only real question you need to ask is: do I need another music player? After all you have a laptop that plays CDs and connects to the internet to download music. As does your telly and probably the toaster. You have a CD player in your house and in your car. Likewise a radio, a digital radio and mobile phone which for no discernible reason also plays music. Not to mention the hi-fi midi system in a box along with your old vinyl at the back of the garage.

WHEELCHAIR ACCESS

We all support the right of our disabled citizens to have the same access as the rest of us to vital services such as shops, libraries and lap dancing bars. And we accept that this could involve the construction of a ramp across the entrance to the Boogie Nights Gentlemen's Club which may leave its non-disabled customers shuffling in sideways through the remaining gap. But do we need disabled access everywhere?

Gwynedd Council recently opened an 'all abilities' trackway in the Snowdonia National Park. The £40,000 path is the highest wheel chair access vantage point in Wales. Great news if you're not the one pushing the wheelchair.

Not content with ensuring access to the top of mountains, The Department for Environment, Food and Rural Affairs has decided that kissing gates and stiles should be removed in favour of cattle grids costing hundreds of pound each. This has dismayed farmers, who argue they the gate has been a cheap and practical solution for access through fields with cattle for hundreds of years. John Collen, of the National Farmers' Union, said: 'Where is it all this going to end? A lot

of footpaths crossing fields, moorland and woods are unsuitable for wheelchairs in any case.'

Perhaps it might be sensible to hold a referendum among Britain's disabled citizens to check if they actually want to be left shivering up Mount Snowdon or in the middle of ploughed field.

DRESS CODES

Few things in life can be as silly as a dress code yet we English persist in enforcing them. Is it really important whether a woman wears a short cloak that covers her shoulders after 6 pm? Or that a gentleman should never wear a tailcoat with black tie?

Ever since man first pulled on an animal skin he has been worrying whether he looked too formal or – in company – too scruffy. One can only imagine that within a few years of the discovery of leather, hapless cave folk were being turned away from the tribal feast for wearing informal sandals.

Even today, when no-one in the country wears a tie for anything but court appearances and reading the news there are still clubs you can't get into unless you're wearing one; a short skirt can get you ejected from Henley and you look like a dork in the clubhouse at Lords if you're *not* wearing a blazer.

In America in the 1870s a German-dry goods merchant named Levi Strauss realised that the hard-wearing denim material he used to make tents for gold prospectors might be better used as trousers. He added a couple of brass rivets and overnight rendered all dress codes obsolete because at the end of the day everyone would rather be wearing jeans than a codpiece. In 2004 Americans spent $14 billion on jeans and no more than $75 on top hats, tie pins and spats – perhaps it's time we got the message.

CHURCH OF (MIDDLE) ENGLAND

No-one likes being told what to do, least of all by a bearded left wing religious freak with fewer followers than Stephen Fry's Twitter page. We're not talking about some cult leader here but Dr Rowan Williams, the current Archbishop of Canterbury.

Dr Williams epitomises all that's bad about the outlook of modern religionists. How can anyone who lives in a medieval castle and walks around with a gold cross around his neck that would make a rap star look cheap possibly preach to us about poverty? Similarly how could an institution that has sent millions to die in religious conflicts over the last 2,000 years claim that wars are bad?

Luckily for us, a lifetime in academia has left the current archbishop pretty confused about what he wants. He's pro gay rights but anti gay clergy. He's anti war but pro Muslim. He's pro ecumenical union with Rome but anti the break-up of the Anglican Church.

However he is very clear about ending the free market and being fiercely green – which would mean closing down Westfield and turning the country into a medieval village where we barter turnips and dance around maypoles as an example to the rest of the world. This far sighted policy should bring the country to its knees in about a year and a half. Then the only example we'll be setting is as exemplary domestic staff to our new Chinese overlords.

As the head of the established church, Dr Williams claims to speak for all of us. But as more people watch the *Eastenders* than attend his church on Sunday, would it not be more logical for Phil Mitchell to giving the country spiritual guidance? He'd certainly be more convincing.

BRUSSELS

You couldn't make it up. Thanks to EU regulations governing the hours bus drivers can work, Lilian Brunton – a grandmother from West Yorkshire – has to get off her bus halfway along the 484 bus route. Then go to the back of the queue to get on next 484 to arrive.

And that's not all. Brussels tells us we can no longer lay out a body at a wake as embalming fluids have been withdrawn under a new biocides directive. Nor can we throw tea bags out in waste meant for compost because they comprise a foot-and-mouth risk or let our dogs in the kitchen if we run a bed and breakfast. Speed limits need to be placed on children's roundabouts to bring them in line with their safety-conscious European counterparts.

It seems the only thing that stops idiots in the European Parliament from stuffing themselves with caviar and foie gras all day is their uncontrollable urge to interfere in every single aspect of British life. What business is it of theirs if we drink light ale – we know it's not a diet drink and we don't want to call it pale ale. And we didn't fight a 100-year-war with France for them to re-categorise Kent and Sussex as part of France in their biodiversity database.

It's almost certainly a fact that 89 per cent of people in Britain have absolutely no idea who their MEP is or how he or she was voted in. Besides, what kind of person takes the time and effort to become an elected official only to spend the next five years measuring sausages? It's time we stood up to this Eurocrat madness. Three simple policies – all beer to be served in pints, road measurements in miles and back to the good old imperial system. If it ain't broke why fix it?

ORGANIC FOOD

They say you can't put a price on your health. Unfortunately eco-hippies can and for most of the last decade it's been going up. A hideous coalition of deluded scientists, new-age evangelists and Jamie Oliver has made us believe that if we don't want to be consumed from the colon out by cancer then we have to eat healthily. First you had to lay off the ready meals and eat vegetables. Then you had to eat home-grown seasonal vegetables. Now it's home-grown *organic* seasonal vegetables .

So how does organic food work? Well, the cost of a family pack of string beans grown in a Dutch laboratory, flown to Kenya to be topped and tailed by weeping children then delivered to a freezer in your local

Tesco's is about a quid. A handful of irregularly shaped, mud-coloured bean strands dug out of an allotment and sold to you by a man with a platted beard is about £7. Do the maths – buying organic makes your monthly mortgage payments look reasonable. This would be bad enough however the Food Standards Agency also announced in 2009 that following a study based on 50 years of research, organic food was no better for you than normal food.

Time may show the organic movement to be as much part of the financial excess of the noughties as gold leaf cocktails or Jordan's charlies. As we languish in a recession no-one is going to have the money to spend £14 on a butternut squash grown in Andean mountain earth. The financial legacy of Brown and Darling means we'll be lucky not to end up having to eat each other. So if it comes to it, eat the rich. At least you'll know they're organic.

PETE DOHERTY

Every music fans knows that rock and roll achieved perfection some time around 1975 and pop music ever since has been little more than electronic nonsense dressed up with a trip through mummy's make-up box. So what is the point of Pete Doherty?

Despite the fact that no one has ever bought – or even heard – one of his solo records, the porridge-faced indie troubadour seems to be a permanent fixture in our newspapers. Not a week passes without this self proclaimed artist displaying his delicate creativity by staggering out of another regional crown court with a broken fag between his lips looking to all the world like Terry Pratchett's anorexic younger brother.

A perpetual law breaker for most of the last decade Doherty has probably spent more time in the court that the average judge. He has been jailed twice and charged with over twenty-one separate drug and driving offences – in most cases being released with little more than a fine. In June 2009, while appearing in court in Gloucester for sentencing on yet another drink drive charge, he was re-arrested before he had even left the building and charged with possession of a controlled substance.

While Doherty may see himself as part of a great tradition of rock-and-roll excess, his trilby hats, fleet of untaxed, second-hand Jaguars and derelict East End flat indicate that he owes more to Del Boy Trotter than Del Amitri.

TWITTER

Where else but the interweb would anyone imagine that they could communicate anything remotely sensible in the less that 140 characters? If ever there was a sign of the imminent breakdown of society then the arrival of Twitter is it.

More addictive that crack cocaine and about twice as devastating in its effect on society, Twitter allows every numbskull across the globe to broadcast what they had for breakfast to every other numbskull across the globe. It's a dream come true for all those self-obsessed idiots who were previously restricted to bellowing the minutiae of their dull lives into a mobile phone while standing in the queue at the bank, sitting in the cinema or the quiet carriage of a train.

Despite consisting mainly of inane, misspelled and highly concise commentary on people's moment by moment mood swings, much of the media would have us Twitter is the greatest communications tool since the telephone. However the writer Bruce Sterling was more sanguine when he said: 'Using Twitter for literate communication is about as likely as firing up a CB radio and hearing some guy recite *The Iliad*'.

Not unsurprisingly Twitter is held in most regard by those involved day-to-day in the business of producing hot air – politicians. They have even credited it with the power to topple governments. To give Twitter credit, it has had a significant effect on the process of government, mainly because politicians, researchers and political journalists seem more intent on tweeting about their choice of socks than actually doing any work. American politicians came under fire after 'tweeting' throughout President Obama's inaugural address to Congress while in October 2009 Canadian MP Ujjal Dosanjh was forced to apologise to the floor for improperly 'tweeting about matters that ought not to have been tweeted about' during televised proceedings of a parliamentary committee.

RUBBISH TERRORISTS

The attack on World Trade Centre in New York shook and saddened people right across the world. However all this seems very far from one's mind when trying to board a plane a Heathrow.

There is some comfort in knowing the airlines want us to reach our destination safely. But when you are standing at the back of a queue for security that snakes out of the terminal which consists almost entirely of overweight tracksuited proles, you start to think that you might be happy to take your chances with al-Qaeda.

The reality is that most security measures are instigated not by major terrorist attacks but by the failed and comical efforts of second-division chancers. We have to take our shoes off at the X-ray machine thanks to the efforts of Richard Reid, a former dishwasher, who boarded to a plane to Miami in 2001 with his trainers packed with Semtex. He was apprehended by passengers while trying to light his sweat-soaked Nikes with a match.

You can't drop people off within half a mile of a terminal thanks to a group of Iraqi doctors who, having failed to set off a car bomb in London, drove 400 miles to Glasgow airport to crash their Jeep Cherokee into the departures lounge. Far from bringing down Western society they set themselves on fire and received a kicking from one of the locals for their trouble.

Are we really in clear and present danger from these idiots? Or is this simply natural selection in action?

FACEBOOK

As we get older we come to realise with some relief that there are many people we will never see again. That guy who drank an entire bottle of Blue Curacao and then threw up down the back of the sofa at your 21st birthday party for example. These people should be chalked up to experience and never spoken of again. So it's simply not right that they should try to become your friend on Facebook.

In theory, using Facebook to get in touch with people is a great idea but the reality is that your friends can already get in touch with you. They know where you live and they have your telephone number. This means that Facebook is simply a vast directory of predatory psychopaths from your murky past who have formed an inexplicable attachment to you. Why does that Chinese mathematician that you spoke to once at university want to share pictures of his grossly overweight wife with you? And why is the girl you dumped after she made an effigy of you from her own hair bombarding you with photographs of her recent wedding? The answer to either of these questions can't be good.

This all assumes the people contacting you are who they claim to be. In 2008, the High Court in London ordered one Grant Raphael to pay £22,000 damages after he posted a fake Facebook page on behalf of Mathew Firsht, a former business colleague. Among other things the page claimed that Firsht was gay and untrustworthy in business.

More worryingly in December 2008, the Australian Supreme Court ruled that Facebook could be used to serve court notices to defendants. You have to ask yourself if the vast majority of people on Facebook are people you never want to see again, or people you don't know claiming to be people you never want to see again or people trying to serve papers on you whether it might not be sensible to steer well clear.

HESTON BLUMENTHAL

One in every 10 programmes on television is a cookery show and each of these shows is helmed by a different and more annoying TV chef. To cut it in this new world of blanket foodie coverage, the culinary poster boys have joined TV weathermen and TV gardeners in the desperate search for a hook that would endear them to the square-eyed masses. Some are blotto like Floyd, some are scary like Delia, others are shouty like Gordon but they all agree on one thing: cooking is an art.

So imagine our surprise when a bespeckled Mr Potato Head in a lab coat appeared on our screens to announce that cooking was no longer an art learned via a long apprenticeship under a chain smoking Parisian maestro with a string of convictions for aggravated assault but a cold science that required no more expertise than the assembly of flat-pack furniture.

Perhaps it was the fact that Heston Blumental's entire culinary experience boiled down a single week's work experience in Raymond Blanc's kitchen that allowed him to imagine for one second that anyone wanted to eat bacon ice cream or have their porridge garnished with garden snails.

Undeterred by the obvious, Heston has continued to plough this unusual culinary furrow; freezing vegetables in dry ice, running chilli con carne through MRI scanners and cooking meat for 24 hours in a vacuum stove no hotter than back of a laptop.

He has managed to spawn two restaurants, six books and several television series and he would have got away with it if he'd stuck to applying his 'molecular cooking' techniques to food that nobody ate any more like Black Forest Gateaux and 20 course medieval banquets.

However the proof was most definitely in the pudding in February 2009, when Blumenthal closed his restaurant The Fat Duck temporarily after some 400 customers fell ill after eating there. Initial reports blamed an outbreak of norovirus among the staff; however, a later investigation found the cause to be contaminated oysters.

THE X FACTOR

There's nothing quite as forgettable as an X Factor contestant. Every autumn a new crop arrives on our screens as if on some seasonal migration from the second circle of hell. Whether they're tearfully recounting the significance of their personal journey to a nodding presenter or hammering out a sub-karaoke version of *Unchained Melody* for the gratification of whooping studio audience of their relatives, most of us have used tissues that we have fonder memories of.

A small test. If you were one of the 13 million people who enthusiastically watched last year's finale, try thinking of the name of one of the finalists. Exactly: you can't. Which makes you wonder where they are now. After failed battle against Cliff Richard and a mobile ring tone for the Christmas number one slot they're more likely to be emptying the bilge tanks on a cruise ship than singing on one.

Everybody knows that the only true winner on X Factor is Simon Cowell. He makes money when the show is broadcast and when you call up to vote. The acts are signed to his record label so he makes money when you buy their records; plus (as all the other record companies have to pay him to let their artists appear as guests on the show) he earns even if you don't. That's why he earns about £50 million a year and you still owe DFS for your sofa.

But the audience do get something else from this annual cavalcade of the mentally deranged and talent deluded. The warm glow of knowing that it's not us up there trying to sing a big band version of a U2 song as our colleagues at the chicken plucking plant gleefully look forward to lifetime of abuse they will heap on us when we return to work.

MPS' EXPENSES

Until the summer of 2009 it was unclear to any rational person why someone would choose to become an MP. Before you got a sniff of a seat on *Question Time*, you had spend years canvassing in crime ridden sink estates and campaigning to save C-Diff infested cottage hospitals. That's a lot of effort to secure the world's most insecure job which largely seemed to involve being shouted at by Jeremy Paxman. Indeed most of us assumed that it was the only work someone with a string of failed businesses and a penchant for deviant S&M could get.

But when the expenses scandal broke the scales fell from our eyes. After years of hearing MPs complain that they were underpaid, we discovered that a bog-standard MP was taking home a whopping £64,000 a year to sit and make gurgling noises on the green benches. MPs also had access to subsidised bars and restaurants twenty-four hours a day, a final salary pension and were even exempt from the congestion charge.

But all these outrageous perks paled into insignificance when compared to MPs expenses claims. This self regulated system has allowed MPs to pay generous salaries to friends, spouses, relatives and hired help whether they actually worked for them

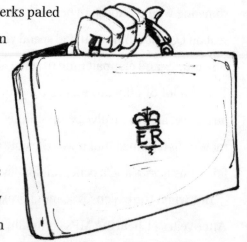

or not. They could pay off mortgages on homes they didn't live in and no tax on those they did. Others simply used the cash to do up stately homes, pimp out bachelor pads with the latest techno gizmos or commission high end accommodation for their pet fowls.

The extraordinary depth and enthusiasm of MPs' abuse of the expenses system boggled the mind. In the old days the worst an MP might to do was get caught cottaging in his lunch break. Nowadays he's likely to have used his luncheon vouchers to buy an actual cottage.

BANKERS

Anyone with kids knows that there is often a price to pay for leaving them unattended. Walls get drawn on, the TV remote control gets put in the dishwasher and the cat gets set on fire. But it's a small price to pay for an extra ten minutes in bed with the wife.

Usually adults can be left on their own without ending up in A & E but this wasn't the case when the Government gave the banking community the run of the house while they had a ten year lie-in. By the time Mervyn King staggered down in his dressing gown, the bankers had managed to put around £178 billion on the country's credit card.

There are complex reasons for the banking crisis and no doubt we'll all have plenty of time to discuss them after we've been made redundant but one big question still remains... what did bankers do with all money they earned?

In February 2010 it was announced that over 100 bankers at the biggest UK based culprit, RBS, were to receive bonuses of over £1 million. If we're rational we may end up feeling a bit sorry for these poor cash heavy bankers. Every government since Mrs Thatcher has justified banking deregulation by arguing huge profits at the top of the system will trickle down through the rest of the economy. This puts the boys in red braces under huge pressure to spend as much of their ill gotten gains on disposable crap as possible.

In 2002 five bankers from Barclays Capital managed to spend £44,000 on a single meal at Gordon Ramsey's Petrus restaurant.

Perhaps it's no surprise that since the downturn, Gordon has found himself with severe financial difficulties.

So maybe we should stop being so hard on the bankers and encourage them to buy another Porsche or third home in Notting Hill or to pop open that bottle of 1787 Chateau Lafite with their fishfingers. Alternatively they could all go to prison where they belong.

FAT BRITAIN

It used to be the case that you could only see a gigantic, wheezing man in elephant style sweat pants or woman whose calves were so chubby that her trainers looked like ballet pumps in the circus. Nowadays you can't take a trip into town without finding half your seat taken up by a strange buttock on the bus or being forced to jump off the curb as a jiggling mass of flesh on an electric scooter wobbles towards you along the pavement like a spam avalanche. There's no doubt about it – Britain is getting fatter.

A 2005 European Commission report stated that Britons were fatter than our Italian, Spanish and French neighbours. In fact we we're among the heaviest people in Europe with around 13 million of us diagnosed as clinically obese - that's the combined population of Liverpool, Leeds and Sheffield.

This year were expected to go further with a third of all adults and a fifth of their children in the country entering a state of KFC inspired corpulence. The fatist naysayers might warn about the huge strain the growth in our waistbands is placing on the NHS - indeed every day more human walruses alive with cancers, heart disease and type 2 diabetes are being winched from their council flats. But very little has been said about the potential uses of a dietarily challenged population. There are plenty of jobs which require a sedentary body such as tube driver, art gallery attendant or manning a public kiosk in any council building in the country. If all else fails why can't a wall of fat people be used to counteract the rise in sea levels.?

None of us are getting any younger – or any thinner. One day soon we'll all loose sight of our genitals so buy shares in Greggs and get ready to celebrate Britain's fat revolution.